The Missing Man

Alan C. McLean

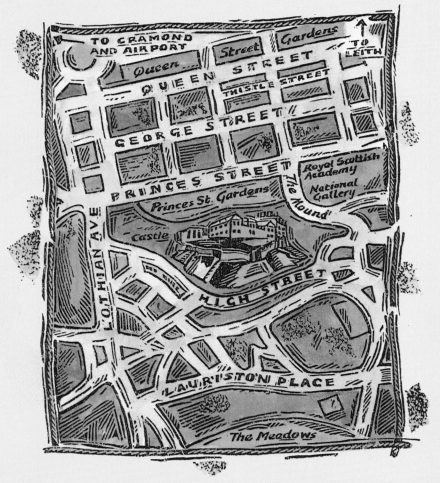

HEINEMANN ELT NEW WAVE READERS

1 AN ART LESSON

It was three o'clock on a hot August afternoon. I had my office
window open and my feet on the desk. I picked up the sign that said
PETER MACARI, Private Investigator and wiped the dust off it.
Business was slow, but that was all right today. I'd had a nice lunch at
the best Italian restaurant in Edinburgh. I'd drunk a little wine and
now I felt sleepy. I liked Edinburgh, capital of Scotland, and usually a
dark, grey town. But today it was nice to look at the view from my
office window. You could see down the hill to Princes Street Gardens.
Crowds of people were sitting on the grass enjoying the sunshine. Next
week, when the Edinburgh Festival started, the crowds would be even
bigger. I felt like joining the people sitting on the grass. You don't get a
lot of sunshine in Edinburgh.

I yawned. The doorbell rang in the outer office.

I heard voices, then Helen looked in from the outer office.

'There's a lady to see you, Mac,' she said.

'Tell her I'm busy,' I said. 'And stop calling me Mac.'

'You'll want to see her, Mac. I know you. I'll show her in.'

Helen was right. She usually is. A tall, slim woman of about thirty,
dressed in a simple black suit and a white blouse walked in.
On the lapel of her suit was a simple gold and diamond
brooch the shape and size of an oyster shell. She
made me feel cheap. I stood up, straightened my
tie and asked her to sit down. She smiled and
thanked me.

'What can I do for you, Miss. . . ?'

'Tebaldi,' she said. 'Here is my card.'

'Well, Miss Tebaldi. . . '

'I need your help, Mr Macari. I
work for a very important art gallery in
Italy. We represent a number of very
important clients. One of our clients'
paintings is. . . ' She hesitated a moment and
touched the brooch on her lapel. 'Let us just
say that this painting is missing. It is a very beautiful painting of the
Madonna by Duccio. We Florentines are very proud of Duccio. He's
one of our greatest painters. I want you to find this painting, Mr
Macari. You will be well rewarded.'

She spoke with a slight foreign accent that was very attractive.

2

She had beautiful black eyes. I looked into them for a moment. Then I had to look away.

'How well?'

'Pardon?'

'How well will you reward me? I don't know much about painting, but I've heard of Duccio. This Madonna must be worth millions of pounds.'

'You are right. The Duccio Madonna is insured for five million pounds. If you find it, I will pay you ten thousand pounds. One thousand now and the rest when I have the Madonna.'

I sat up in my chair and looked at her. 'That's a lot of money,' I said. 'I think you'd better tell me all about this painting of yours.'

Gina Tebaldi crossed her legs - long, slim legs. 'The painting is quite small,' she said. 'About 40 centimetres by 15. It was painted for the Pacellis, one of the richest families in Italy. Barone Pacelli is our client. He owns the Madonna.'

'Barone Pacelli, eh? Very interesting,' I said. 'But why are you looking for this painting in Edinburgh?'

'The Barone agreed to lend the painting to the Royal Scottish Institute. The Institute is organising a special Duccio exhibition for the Edinburgh Festival next week. Two days ago the painting was put on a plane in Rome and flown to Edinburgh. I went to Edinburgh Airport to collect it, but it wasn't on the plane. It wasn't on any other plane from Italy either. Someone has stolen the Madonna, Mr Macari. We want you to find it.'

'Why don't you go to the police?'

The red lips parted, showing perfect white teeth. She smiled. 'The police are - how do you say *imbranato* in English, Signor Macari?'

'I don't know. I'm Scottish. I don't speak Italian.'

'The police are clumsy - they make too much noise. This is a private matter. I want you to find this painting, but I don't want any publicity.' The beautiful mouth closed to a thin red line. She wasn't smiling now.

'Is that clear?' she asked.

'Perfectly clear.'

She counted out a thousand pounds onto my desk. I signed a receipt for the money, then called Helen to show her out.

When Gina Tebaldi had gone, Helen came back in and sat on my desk.

'Well?' she asked.

'Well what? I suppose you were listening to all that.'

'Of course. What did you think of her? Apart from her legs, I mean.'

'Jealous, Helen?'

'Not me. I just don't believe her story. She's no art expert.'

'Oh really?'

'Yes, really. Duccio wasn't a Florentine painter - he was from Siena.'

'Florence, Siena. What's the difference?'

Helen shrugged and got off my desk. 'Okay, don't believe me. Please yourself,' she said, and strolled back into the outer office. I watched her go. She had pretty good legs too.

There's a library just down the road from my office. I walked across to it and looked up a book on Italian art. Helen was right. Duccio was from Siena, not Florence. Now why didn't Gina Tebaldi know that?

4

2 A MEETING WITH THE DIRECTOR

'I'm sorry, but the Director is busy. He can't see you now.' Giles Fanshawe's secretary looked at me over the top of her glasses. She held out my card as if it was dirty. I tried to get up out of the deep leather armchair. It wasn't easy. The Royal Scottish Institute must be doing well if they could afford furniture like this, I thought.

'Can I have a piece of paper?' I asked.

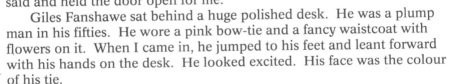

The secretary looked puzzled, but she tore a sheet from her notepad.

I took a pencil from my pocket and drew a Madonna on the piece of paper. I put a halo round the head and wrote *Duccio?* at the bottom. I folded the paper over and gave it to the secretary.

'Give him this,' I said.

She took the piece of paper and went back into Fanshawe's office. A few moments later she returned. She looked even more puzzled than before.

'The Director will see you now,' she said and held the door open for me.

Giles Fanshawe sat behind a huge polished desk. He was a plump man in his fifties. He wore a pink bow-tie and a fancy waistcoat with flowers on it. When I came in, he jumped to his feet and leant forward with his hands on the desk. He looked excited. His face was the colour of his tie.

He held up my drawing of the Madonna. 'Well, Mr Macari, have you got it?' he asked.

I sat down in another deep armchair and lit a cigarette.

'I don't know,' I said. 'Maybe.'

Fanshawe's face grew even pinker. 'Now look here, Macari, I'm not in the mood for games. You sent me this message, didn't you?'

He pushed an envelope across the desk towards me. I stood up and opened it. Inside was a photograph of a painting of a Madonna. In the photograph, the painting was lying on a table. Beside it was a copy of the *Scotsman*, the Edinburgh newspaper, with today's date on it.

I shook the envelope and a piece of paper fell out. A message was pasted on the piece of paper.

I put the photo and the paper back in the envelope and pushed it across Fanshawe's desk. 'I don't have the Madonna and I don't know anything about this note,' I said.

'Come along now, Macari,' Fanshawe said. 'What *do* you know about this, then?'

'I know that the Edinburgh Festival starts next week. I know that you've got a big Duccio exhibition here at the Institute. If the Duccio Madonna isn't in that exhibition, your face is going to be even redder than it is now.'

Fanshawe groaned. 'I know,' he said. 'If Barone Pacelli finds out that the Madonna is missing, he'll never lend the Institute any of his paintings again. He'll probably sue the Institute and I'll lose my job. I'll be ruined.'

'What do you think has happened to it?'

'God knows. It was supposed to arrive in Edinburgh two days ago. It was supposed to be on the flight from Milan. I went to the airport myself to collect it, but it wasn't there.'

'Milan? Did you say Milan?'

'Yes. Why?'

'No, nothing. Are you sure the painting was put on the plane in Italy?'

'Oh yes. I checked that.'

I took Gina Tebaldi's card out of my wallet and gave it to him. 'Do you know this lady?'

'Tebaldi? Galleria Toscana? Never heard of either of them. And I know all the best galleries in Florence.'

I told Fanshawe all about Miss Tebaldi's visit to my office. When I had finished, he looked serious.

'I don't know who Gina Tebaldi is. I don't know if she's working for Pacelli or not. He's never said anything about her. I don't like it.'

'What do you mean?'

'Good God, Macari, don't you read the newspapers? Art is big business today - very big business. The best paintings are worth millions of pounds. There are gangs of thieves who specialise in stealing paintings.'

'But if the paintings are famous, the thieves can't sell them, can they? Everyone will know they were stolen.'

Fanshawe laughed. 'My dear Macari, these paintings are sold to private art collectors. They keep their famous paintings hidden away. There are dozens of rich collectors all over the world who would pay millions of pounds to have that Duccio Madonna on their walls.'

'Do you think Gina Tebaldi is working for one of these private collectors, then?'

'It's possible.'

'You haven't told the police, I suppose.'

'How could we? No one must know the Madonna is missing.'

I stood up to go. 'What are you going to do about the demand for the one million pounds?'

'What can we do? We can't possibly pay it,' Fanshawe replied. 'We haven't got that kind of money.'

'Do you think they really will burn the painting, if you don't pay up?'

'God knows. But we must find it quickly.' He stopped and looked at me carefully. 'I say. You're a detective, Mr Macari. Can't you help us find the Madonna?'

I didn't say anything. I walked to the door.

'The Institute would reward you for your work. Of course, we couldn't pay you what Miss Tebaldi has offered you. But the Royal Scottish Institute - the whole of Scotland, Mr Macari - would be grateful to you.'

I opened the door. Fanshawe's secretary was pretending to be looking at some papers, but she was listening.

I turned back to Fanshawe. 'So it's Mister Macari now, is it?' I said. 'You don't care about the Duccio Madonna. You just want me to save your job, don't you? I've got a lot of questions I want answers to. I want to know who sent you the photo. I want to know who's got the painting now. And I want to know who Gina Tebaldi is working for. But, don't worry, Fanshawe, I'm going to find the missing Madonna. And when I do, then I'll come back here and we can talk about my reward. Until then, goodbye.'

3 THE MAN WITH WHITE GLOVES

'So who do you think has got the Madonna?' Helen asked. We were in my office and she was sitting on my desk again.

'Not Gina Tebaldi, anyway, because we know she's looking for it. By the way, Fanshawe had never heard of her or the Galleria Toscana. She's a fake, all right.' Helen smiled. 'Yes, just like you said.'

'Do you think she's really working for Pacelli?' Helen asked. 'Maybe she's trying to cheat him. Maybe she's really trying to sell the Duccio to one of these international art collectors?'

'But how would she get the painting?' I asked.

'She must have had someone working for her at Edinburgh Airport. Someone who was supposed to steal the painting from the plane and give it to her.'

'But he didn't give it to her.'

'No, he didn't. Instead, he told Tebaldi that the painting wasn't on the plane. He kept the painting himself and sent that message to Fanshawe. When Tebaldi went to the airport to collect the painting, he could say that it wasn't on the plane.'

I thought about Helen's idea for a moment. 'But how did he steal the painting?'

'He must be one of the baggage handlers. They're the only people who touch the baggage between the plane and the terminal. We could always go to the airport and ask my Uncle Willie about it.'

'Your Uncle Willie?'

'Yes. He's the chief baggage handler at Edinburgh Airport.'

'Oh is he?' I asked. I was getting fed up with Helen. She was too clever. I was supposed to be the detective, wasn't I? 'Well, I suppose we'd better go and see what Uncle Willie has to say.'

Uncle Willie had heard nothing about the missing Madonna. I asked if any new baggage handlers had started work recently.

'No,' he said, 'but one of them left yesterday. All of a sudden too. Gavin Baillie was his name.'

'We'd like to speak to him,' I said. 'Where is he now?'

Uncle Willie paused for a moment and looked at Helen.

'Gavin asked me not to tell anyone where he was,' he said.

'Come on, Uncle Willie,' said Helen. 'You can tell us.'

'There was someone else asking about him this morning. A woman. She sounded foreign.'

'Good-looking, young, dressed in expensive clothes?'

'That's right.'

'Did you tell her where he was?'

'No, of course not.'

'Thank God for that,' I said.

Uncle Willie wrote something on a piece of paper. 'Here's Gavin's phone number,' he said.

Helen gave Uncle Willie a hug and kissed him. 'Thanks, Uncle Willie, I knew you would help us.'

He looked embarrassed. 'Don't be silly, Helen. Let me get back to my work.'

Helen and I went off to find the snack bar. Helen got us some coffee while I called Gavin's number. At first Gavin was suspicious and wouldn't talk.

'Listen,' I said. 'You don't want Gina Tebaldi to find out where you are, do you?'

'Tebaldi?' He sounded frightened. 'How do you know about her?'

'She's looking for you, Gavin, and she's not very pleased with you. She thinks you've got something that belongs to her.'

'I'm not frightened of Gina Tebaldi.'

'You should be frightened, Gavin. She's working for some very important people. People like Barone Pacelli. Do you really think you can cheat people like that? You're in big trouble, Gavin.'

There was a pause. Then Gavin said, 'Okay then, I'll talk to you. But it'll cost you. If I tell you where the painting is, you'll have to pay me, okay?'

'We always pay well for good information.'

'A thousand pounds, right?'

'We'll see.'

'Okay. Meet me tonight. There's a pub in Leith called "The Ferryboat". Do you know it?'

'Sure,' I said. 'What time?'

'Ten o'clock. I'll be sitting in the corner. You'll bring the money?'

'Of course, Gavin.' And I hung up.

I went over to the table where Helen was sipping coffee.

'No problem,' I said. 'I'm meeting Gavin tonight. . . '

Helen grabbed my arm. I leant across the table. 'Don't look now,' she whispered, 'but that man at the next table is watching us. He's been listening to your phone call.'

We got up from the table and took the tray back to the counter. I put the coffee cups on the counter and looked back.

10

A good-looking man of about fifty was sitting at the table next to ours. He had silver hair and was dressed in a smart suit. He was reading a paper. His face was deeply tanned and he wore dark glasses. But what really caught my eye were his white gloves. They looked strange, especially on such a hot day.

'He's reading an Italian newspaper,' Helen whispered.

She was right, of course. The newspaper *was* Italian.

'I'm sure he was listening to you when you were talking to Gavin,' Helen said. But she didn't sound so certain now.

I smiled and patted her shoulder. 'You've done very well today, Helen,' I said. 'But don't forget, I'm the detective.'

'God, Macari, I don't know why I work for you.'

'It's because you love me,' I said. 'All women do.'

She swung at me with her handbag. It hit me in the ribs and hurt like hell. But because I was a tough guy, I had to grin and pretend it didn't hurt at all.

4 GAVIN PAYS THE PRICE

And also because I was such a tough guy, I had to go to Leith that night. Leith was Edinburgh's port. Many years ago all the coal from the Scottish coal-mines used to sail from Leith docks. Now the mines were gone and the docks were closed. Most of the pubs where the dockers used to drink were gone too. The pubs that remained were now wine bars and restaurants full of young men in expensive suits making a lot of noise.

'The Ferryboat' was one of Leith's oldest pubs and it hadn't changed a bit. It was dirty-looking outside and dark and smoky inside. It took me a moment or two before I saw Gavin. He was sitting in the corner with a pint of lager in front of him. He wore a black leather jacket over a white T-shirt.

I bought him a whisky to go with his lager. Then he started to talk.

'I know I've been a fool about this painting,' he said. 'But when I had it in my hands, when I had a million pounds in my hands, I thought: "Why should I give it to Tebaldi? Why shouldn't I keep it for myself?"'

'Tebaldi asked you to steal it from the plane?' I asked.

'Yeah.' Gavin laughed. 'It was easy. It was on the Alitalia flight from Rome. All I had to do was to make sure I unloaded the plane. I knew what the painting looked like. I knew it was quite small.'

'Did Tebaldi know someone who wanted to buy the Madonna?'

'I think so,' Gavin said. 'I was going to get a percentage of the money when she sold it. But I thought I'd rather have all the money for myself.'

'So you took a photograph of the painting and sent it off with a ransom note to the Director of the RSI?' I was beginning to understand how it had all happened now.

Gavin looked at me in surprise. 'How did you know about that?' he asked.

'I'm a detective, remember? It's my job to know things like that. Go on with your story. Where's the painting now? Have you still got it?'

'I've got it, but I didn't bring it here. It isn't safe here.'

'Then where is it?'

Gavin shifted in his seat. He tried to look tough, but he only looked scared to me. 'Why should I tell you? What do I get out of it?' he sneered.

I leant over the table towards him. 'Listen, son, you're in a lot of trouble. Tebaldi's looking for you and when she finds you, it won't be funny. She works for some very important people. They want that painting back and they won't wait. If you give it to me, I'll look after it. I won't tell Tebaldi how I got the painting. Then you won't be in trouble any more.'

'What about my percentage?' Gavin asked. 'Tebaldi was going to give me five thousand pounds.'

'I've got five hundred in my pocket for you.'

'You said a thousand!' Gavin protested.

'No, Gavin. You said a thousand. I said "We'll see". This is real money, not talk. When you tell me where the painting is, I'll give you the money. And I won't say anything at all to Gina Tebaldi. Think it over, Gavin. I'm offering you a good deal.'

He pretended to think about it, but he'd already made up his mind. He reached into his pocket and pulled out a piece of pink paper. He pushed it over the table towards me.

'What's this?' I asked.

'It's a Left Luggage ticket from Waverley Station. That's where the painting is. Hand that ticket in at the station and you get the painting. Now what about my five hundred pounds?'

I had the money in a large white envelope. I watched while Gavin counted the money.

'It's not very much,' he complained as he put it into his pocket.

'It's a hell of a lot better than trying to explain things to Gina Tebaldi. You're safe now, Gavin.'

He shrugged. 'Maybe you're right.' Then he grinned. 'This calls for a celebration. Do you want another drink?'

'I'll have a whisky.'

'I'd better go to the Gents first.' And he stood up and headed for the toilets at the back of the pub.

I sat and waited for him to come back with the drinks. I looked at the pink ticket. This piece of paper will buy you five million pounds of the best Duccio, I thought. It was amazing really. When I had the painting, what would I do with it? Hand it back to Fanshawe and the Institute? That's what I ought to do. But Fanshawe would probably just take it and say, 'Thank you, Macari', as if I was a delivery boy. And that would be the end of that. No, I didn't think I'd give it back to Fanshawe. Not at first anyway. I'd let him wait a bit longer for his Duccio. When I had the Madonna, I would have a chat with Gina Tebaldi first. I liked the idea of that. I thought about those dark Italian eyes, those long legs. Yes, I liked the idea of a nice long chat with Gina Tebaldi very much indeed.

I looked at my watch. What had happened to Gavin? I looked around the dark pub. He wasn't at the bar. He was taking a long time in the Gents, wasn't he?

I went into the Gents to look for him. I had a little joke ready: 'Come on, Gavin, stop hiding,' I'd say. 'You're going to have to come out and buy me that whisky.'

But I didn't get a chance to use my joke. Gavin was still in the toilets. I found him in the third cubicle along. When I pushed open the door he was sitting staring up at me. His black leather jacket was unzipped and his T-shirt wasn't white any more. It had gone a funny shade of red from the neck down to the waist. Beneath the blood, I could just make out the long white cut across his throat.

I leant forward and closed his eyelids.

'Poor kid,' I said to him. 'You wanted to play games with the big boys. And look what happened. It wasn't a game after all. You never learnt that, did you?'

But Gavin just sat there and didn't say anything.

14

Fortunately, I knew Inspector Simpson. He was a big, red-faced man who'd been in the Edinburgh Police for more than twenty years. I told him I hadn't got anything to do with Gavin's murder. I told him I was working on a case and I couldn't say anything about it. I did say that I was working for Giles Fanshawe, though.

Simpson kept me at the police station for three hours, asking the same questions time and again. Finally he gave up.

'So you're still going to look for whatever it is you're looking for?' he asked.

'That's right, Inspector.'

'And you're not going to tell me who or what you're looking for?'

'That's right, Inspector.'

'If you do find anything, you will tell us, won't you?'

'You know me, Inspector. I'm always ready to help the police.'

Simpson glared at me. 'I know you all right, Macari. You think you're bloody clever. But you're not as clever as you think. One of these days you're going to need our help.'

'If you say so, Inspector.'

'So I'm going to give you something to help you if you do find the man who killed Gavin Baillie.' Simpson paused. 'Or if he finds you first.'

'Do you mean a gun, Inspector? I hate guns. I never carry them.'

'No, Macari, I don't mean a gun. This is something else, something much more useful. Come down to our technical department and I'll show you.'

It was three o'clock in the morning before I got home. I couldn't sleep. Whenever I closed my eyes I saw Gavin staring up at me.

I went to the office early, but Helen was there before me. She was on the phone.

'Yes, Mr Fanshawe,' she was saying. 'No, I'm sorry, Mr Fanshawe.'

She put her hand over the telephone mouthpiece and made a face at me. 'This is the third time Fanshawe's rung this morning,' she whispered.

I held out my hand and took the phone.

'Good morning, Mr Fanshawe,' I said. 'What can I do for you?'

Fanshawe sounded very angry. Furious, in fact.

'Now look here, Macari, what's going on? What the devil did you mean by giving the police my name last night? I had to go down to the police station at midnight and they kept me there for two hours. Two hours! I was giving a very important dinner party and my guests were not amused. It was all most inconvenient.'

'Yes, well, it was pretty inconvenient for Gavin Baillie too,' I said.

'Who?'

'The boy who was killed last night because of your precious Madonna.'

'That's got nothing to do with me,' Fanshawe replied. 'He shouldn't have got mixed up with criminals. I say,' he went on eagerly,' you haven't found the Madonna yet, by any chance?'

'No, I haven't, Mr Fanshawe. And I haven't decided if I'm going to hand it back to you when I do find it. Bye bye.' And I put the phone down.

Helen looked at me. 'God, you look awful this morning,' she said.

'Thank you, Helen. You really know how to build up a man's confidence.'

'Did the police give you a hard time?' she asked in a softer tone. 'Poor Gavin. Wasn't that terrible?'

'You know, you're the first person who's said a nice word about that kid. Or even given him a thought.' I shook my head and took the pink ticket out of my pocket. I held it up to the light.

'Do you know what this is?' I asked.

'It's a Left Luggage ticket, isn't it?' said Helen.

'That's right. And when I go to Waverley Station and hand this in, the man behind the counter will give me a small packet that's worth five million pounds. That's a lot of money. But is it worth a man's life? I just don't think so.'

'Shall I go and get it for you?' Helen asked.

'Why not?' I replied. 'I need some sleep. Get the painting and then take it to your flat. It'll be safer at your place than here.'

'Don't you want to see the Duccio Madonna?'

'No, I'm fed up with the Duccio Madonna.' I yawned. 'Now I just want to sleep.'

Helen took the pink slip and looked at it.

'I forgot to tell you,' she said. 'I found out something about the man with the white gloves. You know, the man who was watching us at the airport.'

I corrected her. 'The man you *said* was watching us at the airport.'

She ignored me and went on. 'I asked Fanshawe what Barone Pacelli looked like. He described the man at the airport exactly.'

'What about the white gloves?' I asked.

'Apparently, Pacelli has to wear them all the time. His hands were terribly scarred in an accident. There's no doubt about it. The man who was watching us was Pacelli.'

'Okay,' I said, 'it was Pacelli. So what?' I tried to appear casual, but I was worried. I couldn't think what it meant. Why was Pacelli in Edinburgh? It didn't make sense. I was too tired to think clearly.

'Don't you see?' Helen said. 'It means Pacelli is mixed up in the theft of the Madonna. He's looking for it too. And if he thinks that you've got it. . . ' She hesitated. 'Remember what happened to Gavin.'

'Oh, I won't forget that in a hurry,' I replied. 'I was there. I found the body. God, was it only last night?' I put my head in my hands.

Helen came over to me and put her hand on my shoulder. 'Do be careful, Peter,' she said. 'I don't want to lose you.'

I looked up at her. She looked very serious, but her eyes were soft and full of emotion. I felt confused. What was Helen trying to say? I didn't know, so I made a joke out of it. I usually do when I'm scared.

'You'd never find another boss as desirable as me.'

For a moment she kept on looking at me in that same tender way. But now she looked just a little disappointed. Then she laughed and turned away to leave.

'That's right, Mac,' she said as she went out the door. She waved the pink ticket at me. 'And I'd never find a boss who would trust me with a five million pound ticket.'

6 A CALL TO THISTLE STREET

After Helen left, I went home and slept. The phone woke me up. I looked at my watch. It was five o'clock. I picked the phone up. It was Gina Tebaldi.

'Any progress?' she asked.

'Quite a bit,' I said. 'Let's meet and talk about it. Do you know the Central Cafe just off the High Street? I'll see you there in half an hour.'

The Central Cafe looks like something from an American film of the '50s. There's a long chrome bar with smart boys and girls dressed in black and white serving behind it. Behind them is a long glass mirror. I got there early and sat at the bar so that I could watch Gina Tebaldi enter.

'It's very crowded in here,' she said as she sat on the high leather bar stool.

'At least nobody can hear what we say.'

She smiled and smoothed down her tight black skirt. 'True. Now tell me, Mr Macari, have you got the painting for me?'

'No,' I said, 'but I've talked to Gavin.'

There was a pause. She looked down and smoothed her skirt again. When she looked up, her face was expressionless.

'Gavin?' she asked. 'I don't think I know anyone of that name.'

I laughed. 'Very good,' I said. 'You should be on the stage. You're quite an actor.'

Gina Tebaldi ignored my comment. 'What did you talk to this Gavin about?' she asked.

'We started to talk about the painting. Then someone stopped Gavin talking. For good.'

'What do you mean?'

So I told her about meeting Gavin in 'The Ferryboat' and then finding him dead in the toilets. I left out one or two details, of course. Like the pink ticket that was worth five million pounds. When I was finished, she looked frightened. She wasn't acting now.

'But that's terrible. Who could have killed him?'

'I was going to ask you the same question.'

She looked angry now and her eyes flashed. But she was very dignified, still very much the lady.

'Surely, Mr Macari, you don't think I had anything to do with a murder?'

'No? It must have been your boss then.'

She looked up sharply. There was fear in her eyes.

'My boss?'

'That's right. You know, Pacelli. You do still work for him, don't you? Or are you trying to cheat him out of his painting and sell it for yourself?'

'Is Barone Pacelli here in Edinburgh? Have you seen him?'

I told her about Pacelli watching Helen and me at the airport. When I'd finished, she didn't look frightened any more. She was calm.

'You should be careful, Mr Macari,' she said. 'Barone Pacelli is a dangerous man. I know him well. If he has killed Gavin, he will not be afraid to kill you. If he thinks you have the painting, that is.'

'But I told you. I don't have the painting.'

'I hope not, Mr Macari. For your sake.'

'Perhaps you should be careful too, Miss Tebaldi,' I said. 'If Pacelli thinks you have the painting. . .'

Gina Tebaldi smiled and got down from the bar stool. 'It seems that we both have to be careful, Mr Macari. Goodnight.' And she pushed through the crowd and out of the Central Cafe.

I stayed on and had another drink. I wanted to think things over. I started with what I knew. Gavin was dead. Killed by Pacelli? Probably. But what was Pacelli doing in Edinburgh? It was his painting that had been stolen. Perhaps he wanted to have it stolen, I thought, then he could claim the insurance money. Five million pounds. A lot of money. I sipped my drink and thought a bit more about the money. Yes, five million pounds is a lot of money - but ten million is a lot more. Twice that, in fact. Suppose that Pacelli had ordered his painting to be stolen so that he could claim back the insurance money. And suppose that he wanted to get the painting back so that he could sell it again. He could sell it to one of those rich art collectors in America that Fanshawe had told me about. Then his painting would be worth ten million pounds to him, not just five. That was a clever idea. Maybe it was worth killing someone like Gavin Baillie to make it happen.

I felt excited. I wanted to get out of the bar, to get some fresh air. It was too noisy, too crowded in there.

I pushed my way out and turned left up the High Street, up the hill that leads to Edinburgh Castle. It was quiet at this time of day. I stood at the Castle wall and looked down on the old grey town. It was just getting dark and the lights were coming on.

I thought about Gina Tebaldi. Was she working for Pacelli? It seemed unlikely. She had looked really frightened when I mentioned his name. Maybe she had worked for Pacelli before, but now she was working on her own. She had wanted to get the painting for herself. If so, she was in just as much danger from Pacelli as I was. I didn't like that. After all, I was working for her. I had taken her money. And I was a detective. It's not good business to let your clients get killed.

The important thing, I realised, was to avoid Pacelli - at least until I decided what to do with the painting. Helen would have it now. Yes, Helen. I thought of the way Helen had looked at me this morning. I shook my head. I didn't want to think of that. Not just now.

I decided to call in at my office on the way home. The light was on when I opened the door. That was unusual. Helen was always very

careful about putting out all the lights before she left. But inside the office, things were even more unusual. It was a mess. Files were all over the floor, the desk drawers had been forced, the door of the wall safe was hanging open. A couple of photos on my desk had been smashed and my cassette recorder was lying in pieces on the floor. 'Pacelli,' I thought. 'I should call the police.'

I had my hand on the phone when it rang. It was Gina Tebaldi. Her voice wasn't calm now. She was screaming with fear.

'Peter? Help me! Pacelli has got me. He's going to kill me!'

'Where are you?' I shouted.

'Thistle Street. Forty-three. Come quickly, please. He's - aaaahhh!'

Her scream was cut short and the phone was slammed down. Somehow I didn't think she had slammed it down herself.

Thistle Street is in the New Town of Edinburgh, where all the lawyers and doctors live. Thistle Street is one of the narrow back streets that hide between the bigger streets like George Street and Queen Street. I got a taxi and told the driver to drop me at the corner of Thistle Street. I wanted to approach number forty-three on foot. I crept along the dark alley and tried to read the numbers on the doors. Thirty-seven, thirty-nine, forty-one. . . There was no forty-three. Where forty-three should have been, there was only a gap between two houses. But surely this was the place? Gina Tebaldi had said forty-three, hadn't she?

I decided to go back to the corner of the street and start again. Then I heard footsteps behind me. I turned, but I was too slow. There was a flash of white and then something hard and heavy struck the back of my head. I grunted and fell to my knees. Then I heard a voice, a voice that I knew.

'You fool,' the voice said. 'You've hit him too hard. Now he'll never tell us where it is.'

It was a familiar voice, but whose? Just before everything went black, I recognised it. There was no mistake. It was the voice of Gina Tebaldi!

7 NO HERO

When the car door opened, the cold air woke me up. The back of my head was aching. It felt as if a dozen little men were beating it with hammers - giant hammers. I groaned and put my hand up to touch it. A deep voice I hadn't heard before laughed. It wasn't a nice laugh. I opened my eyes very slowly. I was cramped in the back of a sports car. The little men continued their hammering.

The man with the white gloves was looking at me over the back of the driver's seat. Gina Tebaldi was sitting beside him.

'So,' Pacelli said. 'You are not dead, Signor Macari. Gina will be so pleased. She was worried about you. But I am afraid you will be dead soon if you do not help us.'

I struggled to speak. When I opened my mouth, the words came out very slowly. My voice sounded very far away. 'You mean, dead like Gavin?' I asked.

Pacelli raised an eyebrow. 'Gavin?' he asked. 'Was that the name of that stupid boy? What a shame. He thought he was so clever, Signor Macari. He thought he could cheat us. But he was wrong. And so he had to die. I hope you will not make the same mistake, Signor Macari.'

'If you have the painting, let us have it quickly.' Gina Tebaldi's voice was like steel - cold and hard. 'Or you will die.'

'So you're working for Pacelli again?' I asked. My voice still sounded far away. 'Does he know you tried to cheat him?'

Pacelli laughed again. 'Gina and I have settled our differences,' he said. 'Now we are friends again. Is that not so, Gina?'

Gina Tebaldi didn't say anything. She looked at me for a moment then she turned her head away.

I sat up and looked out of the car window. It was dark and there was a cold Edinburgh wind blowing. I could just see the outline of a familiar hill against the sky. The lights of the city glowed in the distance. We were in Holyrood Park, a beautiful wild place in the daytime, but a place of fear at night. The hill was Arthur's Seat. During the day, hundreds of tourists climbed it for the view of Edinburgh. But now it was deserted. Nobody would hear my cries, nobody would come to rescue me here. I shivered and it wasn't just because of the cold.

Pacelli saw me shiver and laughed again. 'I think Signor Macari will help us now,' he said. 'But if he still prefers to be foolish, this may persuade him.'

There was a click and then a knife glinted in his white-gloved hand.

23

He laid the knife against the side of my face. I could feel the blade against my cheek. And then Pacelli twisted the knife the tiniest bit and I felt the blade cut my face. The blood ran down my cheek and onto the collar of my shirt. I looked at Pacelli. He was grinning. 'My God,' I thought, 'he's enjoying this.'

'Well, Signor Macari,' he said. 'Are you ready to help us now?'

In books this is when the hero shouts, 'No, never! I'll never tell you! You'll have to kill me first!' But this wasn't a book and I'm no hero. So what I said was, 'Okay, Pacelli. Let's go and get your Madonna.'

Pacelli looked disappointed. No more knife work for him that night. He looked at me with dislike.

'Wipe your face,' he said. 'It's bleeding.'

'Here,' Gina Tebaldi said, pulling a handkerchief from her handbag. 'I'll do it.' And she started to wipe the blood away. I jerked my face away from her and she stopped.

After that, it was soon done. I took them to Helen's flat. She gave me the painting. It was a small packet wrapped in brown paper. Helen and I watched as Pacelli ripped the paper off and glared at the painting. It was a small yellow-and-red painting. The colours were dull. There were tiny holes in the wood. Pacelli examined the front and back closely. Then he smiled, a happy, contented smile this time. He held the painting up and kissed it.

'At last,' he said. '*Madonna mia*, you have come back to me.'

Gina Tebaldi stood beside him, looking on. There was still no expression on her face. I had no idea what she was thinking.

Pacelli took hold of her arm. 'And now, my dear,' he said, 'we have to say farewell to these charming people. Do not try to stop us, Signor Macari, or phone the police. It will be useless. *Addio.*'

'*Arrivederci*,' I replied.

'No, Signor Macari. We say *arrivederci* in Italian only when we are going to meet someone again. I am afraid we are not going to meet again.'

I shrugged. 'Miss Tebaldi knows I don't speak Italian,' I said.

With a bow to Helen, Pacelli left, still holding Gina Tebaldi by the arm.

When they had gone, Helen looked at me. 'Is that it, then?' she asked. 'You're just going to let them go. You're going to let them get away with it?'

'They would have killed me, Helen,' I protested. 'You wouldn't want that, would you?'

'But there must be something we can do to stop them.'

'There is,' I replied. 'Wait.'

I picked up the phone and dialled.

'Inspector Simpson?' I said. 'Pacelli and Tebaldi have got the painting. . . Yes, I did what you said. You should be receiving the messages now. . . They're in a red sports car. . . Good. Let me know when you find them. I want to be there. . . Bye.'

'When I was at the police station last night Simpson gave me a bug - a little electronic transmitter. It sends out a signal to the car. The police can work out where the car is and where it's heading. It's sending out signals now, you see.'

Helen smiled at me and put her arms around my neck. 'You clever thing, Macari,' she said. 'And I thought you were letting them escape.'

She started to kiss me, then she looked at my cheek and frowned. 'What happened to your face?' she asked.

'I cut myself shaving,' I replied.

'But. . .'

The phone interrupted her.

'Yes, Inspector Simpson. Cramond? Yes, I know where that is. I'll see you there in fifteen minutes.'

I put the phone down and threw my arms around Helen.

'Come on, Helen,' I said, 'the bug has worked. The police have caught them. Let's go!'

8 THE END OF THE ROAD

By the time Helen and I got to Cramond, it was almost all over. As we drove down the narrow streets of the village, we could see the blue lights of police cars flashing against the night sky. A couple of young policemen were keeping the small crowd back from the scene. But when I mentioned Inspector Simpson's name, one of them let us through.

'He's over there,' the policeman said, pointing to the car nearest the sea wall.

Simpson was standing in front of a police car looking down at the sea. There were black skid marks on the road and part of the sea wall was broken.

'What happened?' I asked him. 'Did you get them?'

'We've got Tebaldi back there.' Simpson nodded at the car behind him.

'What about Pacelli?' Helen asked.

'We were too late for him, I'm afraid,' he said and pointed down at the sea. I looked over the sea wall. The sports car lay on the rocks below. It had hit them head on and the front of the car was smashed. Two ambulancemen were down there trying to pull something out of the driver's seat. Something that had once been a man. I saw a white-gloved hand hanging out of the car window. Then I turned away.

'Our little bug worked perfectly,' said Simpson. 'We picked them up on our screen at the police station immediately. They were heading north. We caught up with them just outside Cramond. A Ferrari's a fast car - a lot faster than any of our police cars - but Pacelli didn't know where he was going. He didn't know that the road ends at Cramond. After that, there's nothing but the sea.' The inspector smiled grimly. 'It was the end of the road for him all right.'

'Well, he did kill Gavin Baillie,' Helen said.

'Oh, I'm not shedding any tears for Barone Pacelli,' the inspector continued. 'The Italian police were after him too. They knew what game the Barone was playing. Pacelli wanted to have his painting stolen. Then he could claim the insurance money. And when he got the painting back again, he could sell it to some rich American collector. That way he'd get ten million pounds for the painting, instead of five million.'

'What about Gina Tebaldi?' I asked.

'The Italian police told us all about her too. They want her for handling stolen paintings.' He paused and looked at me for a moment. 'She's over there. She wants to talk to you,' he said.

'Peter. . .' Helen began.

I squeezed her hand. 'It's okay, Helen. I can handle this. She's got a right to talk to me. She's my client, remember?'

I walked over to the police car. The policeman sitting beside Gina Tebaldi pushed a button and the car window slid down. I looked in.

'Are you all right?' I asked. It was a silly thing to say, but it was all I could think of at the time.

'Yes, thank you, Mr Macari,' she replied. She spoke quite calmly, as if we were chatting over a cup of tea. Or a drink in the Central Cafe, I thought.

'I owe you an explanation,' she said.

'You were working for Pacelli all the time, weren't you?'

'No, not all the time. At first I thought I could cheat him. I thought that when Gavin got me the painting I could sell it in America. I know some collectors there.'

'But when you found out that Pacelli was here in Scotland, you were afraid.'

She smiled. 'Pacelli is a very important man in Italy. He has lots of friends. I realised it was a mistake to try and cheat him. It was more sensible to work with him than against him.'

'You should have told me the truth, you know. I was working for you.'

'The truth?' she asked. 'But then you wouldn't have helped me, would you?'

'But I didn't help you.'

'Oh yes, you did, Mr Macari. And I'm grateful.'

'Grateful? What for?'

'For finding Gavin, for getting the painting for us. You found the Madonna, Mr Macari. And then you gave it to us, don't forget.'

And with that, she pushed the button and the window slid up. The police car drove away.

I just stood there. Then I heard a loud voice behind me.

'Now look here. I don't care who's dead and who's alive. I want my painting. I insist on it. You don't understand who I am. I am Giles Fanshawe, the Director of the Royal Scottish Institute. I demand that the Duccio Madonna is returned to me.'

Simpson spoke very quietly. 'I've told you already, Mr Fanshawe. We have not yet recovered the painting. When we do find it, we will return it to its rightful owner.'

'That's me, dammit!' Fanshawe roared. 'This is outrageous. I demand to speak to the officer in charge!'

'I am Inspector Simpson of the Edinburgh Police. I am the officer in charge. I have to tell you. . . '

Simpson was interrupted by one of his policemen. He was holding something in his hands.

'Excuse me, Inspector,' the policeman said, 'but one of the ambulancemen found these in Pacelli's car. What shall I do with them?' And he held out half a dozen pieces of brown wood.

Fanshawe recognised them at once. In the blue light of the police car, his face went a deep shade of purple. I thought he was going to explode.

'The Madonna!' he screamed. 'It's the Duccio Madonna! Let me see it.'

Fanshawe seized the pieces of wood out of the policeman's hands. 'My God, what have you done to it? It's broken, ruined. What am I going to do when the exhibition opens next week?'

'It couldn't be. . . repaired. . . before then, sir?' Simpson asked.

'Of course it couldn't, you idiot,' Fanshawe shouted. 'This isn't a tea-cup! The restoration of works of art is a highly skilled job. The Madonna can't be repaired. It's worthless now.'

'Well, anyway, sir,' Simpson said, 'you'd better keep these. The painting is yours, as you said.'

But Fanshawe was looking at the fragments closely. He took out a small magnifying glass and put it to his eye. There was silence as he studied the pieces of wood. Then he put the magnifying glass back in his pocket and looked around him. He looked dazed. Then he smiled.

'The old devil,' he said. 'The crafty old devil.'

'What's the matter?' asked Helen.

'It's a fake. The wood is new. This is a copy of the Duccio.'

'Then where is the real Duccio?' asked Simpson.

'God knows,' replied Fanshawe, handing the fragments back to Simpson.

'Probably still in Pacelli's castle in Italy.'

'What about the reward?' I asked, as Fanshawe turned to go.

'Reward?' he asked. 'What reward?'

'You told me there would be a reward if I found the painting. Well I found it. So what about the reward?'

'My dear fellow,' Fanshawe said, 'the reward was offered for the Duccio. This isn't the Duccio. You can hardly expect the Royal Scottish Institute to pay you for finding a fake. These fragments of wood are worthless. For all I care, you can keep them. Goodnight.' And Fanshawe walked away towards his car.

'Well?' Simpson said when Fanshawe had gone. 'Do you want these?'

Helen held out her hand. 'Yes,' she said. 'We'll take them as a souvenir.'

'I'm afraid you haven't got very much for your work on this case,' said Simpson, handing the fragments to Helen.

'No,' I replied. Then I remembered. 'But I've still got the five hundred pounds left of the money Gina Tebaldi gave me.'

'No you haven't,' said Helen.

'I haven't? Why not?'

'Because I've spent it.'

'You've spent five hundred pounds? What on?'

'On a holiday for two. I bought the tickets this morning.'

'A holiday? Where?'

'In Siena, of course. Then we can see some real Duccios. I hear they have some marvellous paintings in the cathedral there. And then there's the wine and the wonderful Italian food. You need to get away, Peter. You need to get back to your Italian roots.'

'I've told you before, Helen. I'm not. . .' Then I stopped. Something had just occurred to me. 'You said you had bought two tickets.'

'That's right. One for you and one for me. I've booked us a room at the Hotel Toscana, Siena.'

'You mean. . .' I began.

'God, you are stupid sometimes, Macari,' Helen said, putting her arms around my neck and kissing me. 'You didn't really think you were going to get rid of me as easily as that, did you?'

'No, I suppose not,' I replied. What else could I say?

STORY POINTS

Chapter 1
1 How much is the Madonna insured for?
2 How much does Gina Tebaldi offer Macari to find the Madonna?
3 Why does Helen think that Gina isn't an art expert?

Chapter 2
4 How does Macari persuade Fanshawe to see him?
5 Which flight was the Madonna supposed to be on?
6 Is the Royal Scottish Institute going to pay £1million?

Chapter 3
7 How does Gavin offer to help?
8 Where does he tell Macari to meet him?
9 Who do you think the man in the white gloves is?

Chapter 4
10 Who sent the ransom note to the Royal Scottish Institute?
11 Where is the painting?
12 What happens to Gavin?

Chapter 5
13 How does Inspector Simpson help Macari?
14 Who collects the painting?
15 What is the name of the man who was listening to them at the airport?

Chapter 6
16 How does Gina react when Macari tells her that Pacelli is in Edinburg
17 Where does Macari go to think things over?
18 Who asks Macari to go to Thistle Street?

Chapter 7
19 Where does Macari wake up?
20 How does Pacelli persuade Macari to give him the painting?
21 How do the police keep track of Pacelli's car?

Chapter 8
22 What happened to Pacelli's car?
23 What happened to Gina Tebaldi?
24 What's wrong with the painting?